OASIS
PAGES

OASIS PAGES

Teen Writing Quest
Find Your Daily Writing Habit

THE
collective
BOOK STUDIO

Everyone has important things to say.

—Grace Welker, creator of the Oasis Pages

These pages belong to

_____

If you do not have permission,
you should not be reading them.

PRIVATE

WELCOME

The Oasis Pages Quest invites you to set out on a daily writing journey. All you have to do is follow the road map and write. You'll find a variety of interesting and supportive templates and cues for sparking your curiosity and engaging in a personal writing habit—whether this is your first time or you've been writing for years.

Turn the page to begin the journey into the oasis . . .

THE MAP

This book has been designed as a writing journey, filled with pages to get you thinking about your life and your writing routines in new ways. The goal is to write daily for two to three months.

Orientation

Get Oriented 10-13

Find out what it's all about.

Get Resourced 14-17

Prepare for your Oasis Pages quest.

Get Started 18-35

Explore the About Me pages and start writing yourself down. You'll also discover Writing Superpower #1.

The Quest

Begin Page-a-Day Writing 36-111

These pages are the heart of your writing journey. Plan to spend about fifteen minutes a day writing for about two months.

The following signposts along the way will help guide you on your journey:

- ✏️ Specialized Templates
- ✏️ Prompts & Tips
- ✏️ Pause Days
- ✏️ Superpower Pages
- ✏️ Inspiring Quotes
- ✏️ Free Writing Spaces

Congratulations! 112-117
A quest always ends with a celebration, as well as some time to reflect, take stock, and figure out what you learned and what comes next.

At the end of your journey, you'll have a book of your life and, ideally, a daily writing habit. The real magic about quests are the inner rewards, which are unique to each person.

Keep On Writing

Notebook 118-153
Use these open-space pages at any time throughout the quest—or save them until the end to experiment and personalize your approach.

Bonus Resources

Jump-Starters 154-157
Good advice, creative invitations, and concrete ideas for writing and life—plus a go-to page of cues to get you writing any time.

GET ORIENTED
The Basics

OASIS
an inner feeling of comfort,
no matter what's going on around you

WHAT IT FEELS LIKE WHEN YOUR WRITING HABIT IS AN OASIS:

✓ You want to write.

✓ You remember to write.

✓ You have everything you need to write (pens, paper).

✓ You find or create time to write.

✓ You enjoy it.

✓ You write even when you don't enjoy it.

✓ Writing helps you in ways that matter.

✓ You do it for you.

Writing can provide a space of personal refuge, away from outer pressures and messages, where we can hear ourselves think. Across time, all over the planet, people from all walks of life write down their thoughts, encounters, emotions, and the ins and outs of their daily lives—for no one but themselves. A regular writing practice like the Oasis Pages can support the navigation and integration of life experiences, empower self-learning, and support you when the pages are filled.

What I think about when I think about an oasis _____

_____

_____

_____

_____

_____

_____

_____

_____

_____

_____

PAGES

an interactive space for creating and communicating
through words, pictures, colors, shapes

The Oasis Pages are for you to fill, to express, and to discover yourself through a variety of prompts and ideas. Whatever your life experience, no matter how hard or how easy, you have important things to say. No one else has your body, your mind, your heart, your interests, your bottom lines. Make every page your own.

QUEST
a personal journey with an intended goal or destination,
along with the drive and willingness to rise to the challenge

OASIS PAGES QUEST GOAL:
Write daily in these pages for two months.

Plan for fifteen minutes a day—feel free to spend more (and, of course, sometimes less). Maybe you write all the time and are looking for new ideas for what to write. Maybe you wrote when you were younger but now think it's boring or too slow. Writing by hand is definitely slower than typing, but it can be anything but boring.

My past and current personal writing habit is _____
_____
_____
_____
_____
_____
_____
_____

I SAY YES TO THE QUEST.

Today's date: _____

[Signature/Doodle]

Pause Pages & the Writing Superpowers

All quests have times when stopping becomes the best way forward, looking at things differently or learning something new. Every fourteen pages (about every two weeks), you will be invited to pause and guided to do or write something. Plan to take a couple of days with each of these, and more if you want to.

Pause days are also where you will be introduced to the Writing Superpowers: foundational tools for every writer.

Non-Writing Days

Things happen on a quest because life is always happening. What do you do when you just can't write or need to miss a day? Don't worry about it. You can always jump back in. Rather than let non-writing days discourage you, make you think you're doing it wrong, or inspire you to give up, accept that they are part of the journey.

Just make a plan for when you have more than three days in a row of not writing, so you can get back to writing. Remind yourself why you want to write daily.

A NOTE TO ALL THE REBELS

These are your pages. Use them however you want. Work through them backward or in random order. Don't write daily, or write twice a day or only on a full moon. Create drawings, collages, poems, love letters, song lyrics, sci-fi stories, and comic strips.

GET RESOURCED

OASIS PAGES QUEST GOAL:
Write daily in these pages for two months.

Essentials

When to Write

After school, before school, before bed, at lunch, in between things—write whenever it works for you. It might be the same time every day or change constantly.

Where to Write

Wherever you can. People write in bed, on couches, at desks, in bathrooms, in bookstores, cars, libraries, and in nature. Some people like quiet when they write. Some can write anywhere and even prefer background noise.

When and where I might write _____

_____

_____

_____

_____

Why Write

Everyone writes for different reasons. What are yours?

I want to write because _____

_____

_____

_____

_____

_____

_____

_____

_____

_____

_____

_____

_____

_____

What to Write

Each day will be different. The cues, questions, and prompts are your starting place. Write what interests you. Write the truth. Write what you want to write. What's going on in your life? What are you thinking about? Make lists. Write a letter.

Challenges

Every Quest Has Challenges

And the challenges are different for each person. It could be finding the time, it could be not having enough to say, it could be having too much to say! Whatever your challenges, on a quest, there's only one way to deal with them: Stay focused on your goal.

When the Words Don't Come

Sometimes your pen and your words will flow easily, and sometimes you'll struggle to find the words. Be patient. Write the next word. Write "I don't know what to write." Eventually something will come.

Confidentiality

If you are concerned about sneaky siblings or other overcurious people, ask them to respect your privacy. If someone does read your pages, don't let it keep you from continuing to write.

Things I think might challenge me: _____

_____

_____

_____

_____

_____

_____

_____

_____

What I can do after three or more "non-writing days" to get back to

writing: _____

_____

_____

_____

_____

_____

_____

_____

_____

GET STARTED
About Me

Name _____

Usually called _____

Why I have the name I have _____

_____

_____

_____

Age _____

Birthday _____

How I celebrated my last birthday _____

_____

_____

_____

Where I live _____

Where I was born _____

Time I was born _____

Other facts about my birth _____

_____

_____

Siblings _____

Languages I know _____

_____

Heritage/ancestry _____

_____

_____

_____

Earliest memory _____

_____

_____

_____

_____

Things I'm good at _____

_____

_____

_____

_____

Things I'm not interested in _____

_____

_____

_____

_____

_____

MORE ABOUT ME

My attributes

Circle ten or more words

Outgoing	Independent	Flexible
Shy	Cooperative	Decisive
Private	Friendly	Courageous
Bossy	Quiet	Unreliable
Intelligent	Thoughtful	Questioning
Moody	Curious	Pessimistic
Popular	Sensitive	Rebellious
Methodical	Opinionated	Kind
Creative	Stubborn	Unique
Reflective	Dreamy	Dependable
Judgmental	Active	Obedient
Fair	Easygoing	Solitary
Honest	Boring	Hopeful
Blunt	Realistic	_____
Caring	Reliable	_____
Generous	Trusting	_____
Self-absorbed	Practical	_____
Funny	Unpredictable	

REFLECT:

Do I think other people would describe me the way I see myself?

_____

_____

_____

_____

_____

_____

Are there any attributes I would like to develop? What are they and why?

_____

_____

_____

_____

_____

_____

_____

_____

_____

My Favorite . . .

Season _____

Number _____

Color _____

Food _____

Place _____

Animal _____

Dessert _____

Book _____

Movie _____

Famous person _____

Song _____

Things to do

_____

_____

_____

_____

Things I have

_____

_____

_____

_____

People

_____

_____

_____

_____

THREE WORDS TO DESCRIBE . . .

Places I've visited

_____

_____

_____

Things I'm grateful for

_____

_____

_____

Ways I move my body

_____

_____

_____

My day today

_____

_____

_____

People I trust

_____

_____

_____

My parents

_____

_____

_____

Things I'd like to learn

_____

_____

_____

My weekends

_____

_____

_____

22

23

FIVE WORDS THAT DESCRIBE . . .

My summers

_____

_____

_____

_____

_____

My closest friends

_____

_____

_____

_____

_____

The kind of person I want to be

_____

_____

_____

_____

_____

The kinds of people I don't like

_____

_____

_____

_____

_____

Where I live

_____

_____

_____

_____

_____

Family gatherings/group events

_____

_____

_____

_____

_____

SEVEN THINGS I'VE FELT IN THE LAST WEEK

○ angry

○ happy

○ depressed

○ alive

○ afraid

○ worried

○ good

○ peaceful

○ calm

○ confident

○ anxious

○ accepting

○ ashamed

○ impatient

○ frightened

○ powerful

○ proud

○ resistant

○ sad

○ brave

○ helpless

○ jealous

○ open

○ surprised

○ guilty

○ grateful

○ upset

○ loving

○ concerned

○ relieved

○ curious

○ confused

○ content

○ unhappy

○ bored

○ lucky

○ cursed

○ included

○ unsure

○ reluctant

○ just right

○ optimistic

- ○ stupid
- ○ critical
- ○ joyful
- ○ hopeful
- ○ nauseous
- ○ heavy
- ○ tired
- ○ breathless
- ○ energetic
- ○ jittery

- ○ relaxed
- ○ full
- ○ restricted
- ○ focused
- ○ open
- ○ grounded
- ○ spacey
- ○ alert
- ○ comfortable

BONUS

Each of these words can also be writing prompts:

"In what ways am I _____?"

"What does _____ feel like?"

"An example of _____ was the

time when _____."

26

EVEN MORE ABOUT ME . . .

What I ate for breakfast _____
_____

The last time I swam _____

What I wore yesterday _____
_____

My favorite thing to wear _____
_____

The shoes I usually wear _____

New things I've done in the last year _____
_____
_____

What I value _____
_____
_____

What I think about dogs _____
_____

What I think about cats _____
_____

A highlight from yesterday _____
_____
_____

My biggest fear _____

_____

Things that drive me crazy _____

_____

_____

What I'm obsessed with _____

_____

_____

My ideal future _____

_____

_____

_____

A few things I am curious to know about myself or the world _____

_____

_____

_____

_____

_____

_____

_____

_____

MY LIFE IN ONE SENTENCE A YEAR.

You don't need to write your definitive autobiography, just a broad sketch, things like "Another year in Texas." "Started school. Mr. Thomas." "Baby brother born. Love." Fill in to your current age.

Age 1 _____

Age 2 _____

Age 3 _____

Age 4 _____

Age 5 _____

Age 6 _____

Age 7 _____

Age 8 _____

Age 9 _____

Age 10 _____

Age 11 _____

Age 12 _____

Age 13 _____

Age 14 _____

Age 15 _____

Age 16 _____

Age 17 _____

Age 18 _____

THE SIX-WORD BIO

Write your life in six words. Create a few versions.

Writing Superpower #1

CURIOSITY

Who are you? What is it like to be you? What do you do? What do you know about yourself? These don't have to be deep questions. Some people prefer oranges to apples. Others like plaid. Some people read a lot and some love throwing parties—and some both.

JUMP-STARTERS TO ACTIVATE THE CURIOSITY SUPERPOWER

Curious Body

Curiosity in the body feels relaxed and open and has a spark of aliveness. You can encourage curiosity just by shifting your body state. Try it out: Ask yourself, "What does curiosity feel like?"

Close your eyes. Settle into your body and spend as long as it takes right now to feel what curiosity feels like. Write a few words, images, or notes about the experience.

_____

_____

_____

_____

Remember the feeling, so you can return to it when you write

Curious Mind

It can be a challenge to awaken curiosity when we're tired or overloaded. Curiosity in the mind is an outlook, a choice. Whenever you need a spark for your writing, ask yourself, "What is something I want to say right now?"; "What do I really think about broccoli?"; "When was the last time I shared a secret?"; "What are my associations with the color orange?"

Use the questions in the pages of this book and make up your own.

Curious Heart

We all have good reasons to want to protect our hearts at times, but curiosity comes alive when we are willing to be vulnerable, wondering, asking, and to risk not knowing. In our personal writing pages, we can cultivate a curious heart by expressing freely and fully the unique, quirky ways we see the world, the people we encounter, and, most important, the specific ways we love the world.

CURIOSITY SUPERPOWER PAGES

Use these pages to explore your Curiosity Writing Superpower
with one or two of the Jump-Starters on the previous page
or however you want.

There is only one good reason to write—because you want to.

day of the week _____ date _____ time _____

location _____ weather _____

How I feel right now: _____

_____

_____

What I want to say right now: _____

_____

_____

_____

_____

[freespace] _____

_____

_____

_____

_____

_____

_____

_____

Word for the day: _____

One of the best memories I have is: _____

_____

_____

_____

_____

_____

_____

_____

_____

_____

_____

_____

_____

_____

_____

_____

_____

_____

_____

_____

_____

From the earliest times, humans have made marks of some kind, drawing, writing, etching things that mattered to them.

day of the week _____ date _____ time_____

location _____ weather _____

How I feel right now: _____
_____
_____

What I want to say right now: _____
_____
_____
_____
_____

[freespace] _____
_____
_____
_____
_____
_____
_____
_____

Word for the day: _____

A typical day in my life: _____

_____

_____

_____

_____

_____

_____

_____

_____

_____

_____

_____

_____

_____

_____

_____

_____

_____

_____

Don't worry about getting anything "right." There is no such thing as "right" in your personal pages. Enjoy the writing. Share details. Be specific. Imagine telling someone who is really interested in what you're saying.

day of the week _____ date _____ time_____

location _____ weather _____

How I feel right now: _____

_____

_____

What I want to say right now: _____

_____

_____

_____

_____

[freespace] _____

_____

_____

_____

_____

_____

_____

_____

Word for the day: _____

The last thing that really disappointed me: _____

_____

_____

_____

_____

_____

_____

_____

_____

_____

_____

_____

_____

_____

_____

_____

_____

_____

_____

_____

Writing at more or less the same time every day helps most people keep up a daily habit.

day of the week _____date _____time_____

location _____weather _____

How I feel right now: _____

_____

_____

What I want to say right now: _____

_____

_____

_____

_____

[freespace] _____

_____

_____

_____

_____

_____

_____

_____

Word for the day: _____

What makes me mad? _____

_____

_____

_____

_____

_____

_____

_____

_____

_____

_____

_____

_____

_____

_____

_____

_____

_____

_____

_____

_____

_____

_____

 If you like to write, read.

day of the week _____date _____time_____

location _____weather _____

How I feel right now: _____

_____

_____

What I want to say right now: _____

_____

_____

_____

_____

[freespace] _____

_____

_____

_____

_____

_____

_____

_____

Word for the day: _____

How am I similar to my friends? How am I different? _____

_____

_____

_____

_____

_____

_____

_____

_____

_____

_____

_____

_____

_____

_____

_____

_____

_____

A daily writing habit or practice is truly as unique as the person who writes—whether you're recording everyday events, emotions, descriptions of nature, the details of a recent experience, or any other thing you want.

day of the week _____date _____time_____

location _____weather _____

How I feel right now: _____

_____

_____

What I want to say right now: _____

_____

_____

_____

_____

[freespace] _____

_____

_____

_____

_____

_____

_____

_____

_____

Word for the day: _____

12

When I was younger, _____

_____

_____

_____

_____

_____

_____

_____

_____

_____

_____

_____

_____

_____

_____

_____

_____

_____

_____

_____

_____

 Write down everything that happens when you go somewhere new, whether it's close by or a big trip. Changes and new experiences provide fresh perspectives. Write the details you'll enjoy rediscovering later.

day of the week _____ date _____ time_____

location _____ weather _____

How I feel right now: _____
_____
_____

What I want to say right now: _____
_____
_____
_____

[freespace] _____
_____
_____
_____
_____
_____
_____
_____

Word for the day: _____

14

A few of my quirky habits: _____

_____

_____

_____

_____

_____

_____

_____

_____

_____

_____

_____

_____

_____

_____

_____

_____

_____

When you get stuck on what you want to say, just write one word, then another.

Pause & Look Around

QUEST GOAL REMINDER:
Write daily in these pages for two months.

It's been a week or two since you began. Take a moment to reflect on what you've learned and experienced so far. How's it going? Are you finding your writing rhythms? Did you take any non-writing days? Do you need anything to make it easier to write daily?

_____

_____

_____

_____

_____

_____

_____

_____

_____

_____

_____

_____

_____

_____

Write down some of your successes in writing and life recently.

Writing Superpower #2

THE BODY

The body is a writer's best friend and a generous source of prompts, questions, language, stories, and experiences. All we need to do is get curious and listen. Not all of what we find may be comfortable at first, but without a partnership with our bodies, our writing will suffer and likely we will too.

JUMP-STARTERS TO ACTIVATE THE BODY WRITING SUPERPOWER

Body Check-In

When you sit down to write, check in with your head, your heart, and your belly. Choose one word or phrase to express what you find. It could be anything: a noun, an adjective, a verb, a place, an image. If this is difficult, that's OK. Keep at it. The more often you check in, the more articulate you can become in describing your inner landscapes.

Sense Writing

Try writing from one of your senses. You can do this exercise on its own or as part of your daily writing. Relax for a moment, choose one of the senses, and then write down everything you hear, see, or feel on your skin. Smell and taste can be harder—try writing about a recent meal or the kinds of smells you like.

A Short History of My Body

Turn your body into a character: What kinds of things has your body done and seen? Where has it spent time? What does it like? Has it needed any special care? Has it accomplished something you want to remember? Take a page (or more) to write it all down.

"I remember . . ."

The body stores our memories. A great writing prompt for anytime and anywhere is to start with "I remember . . ." Picture yourself, your body experiencing "that time when." Describe everything in detail. When you get stuck, write "I remember" again and keep writing. Continue like this for ten or fifteen minutes.

The body cannot lie.

—anonymous

BODY SUPERPOWER PAGES

Use these pages to explore your Body Writing Superpower
with one or two of the Jump-Starters on the previous page
or however you want.

_____

_____

_____

_____

_____

_____

_____

_____

_____

_____

_____

_____

_____

_____

_____

_____

_____

_____

MY BODY
(Draw)

If you draw, go for it! Otherwise, a stick figure will absolutely work.
You can include shapes, colors, words . . .
it can be impressionistic or realistic or cartoonish.

MY BODY
(Write)

_____

_____

_____

_____

_____

_____

_____

_____

_____

_____

_____

_____

_____

_____

_____

_____

What are your strongest features? Describe your hair, face,
torso, arms, and legs in detail. Do you have any scars?
How do you feel about your body?

56

day of the week _____ date _____ time _____

location _____ weather _____

My head feels _____

My heart feels _____

My belly feels _____

What my body wants to say right now: _____

_____

_____

_____

_____

[sense writing or freespace] _____

_____

_____

_____

_____

Phrase of the day: _____

17

What are the things that make me happiest? _____

_____

_____

_____

_____

_____

_____

_____

_____

_____

_____

_____

_____

_____

_____

_____

_____

_____

_____

_____

Writing by hand slows us down to the rhythms of the body, so we can hear what we're really thinking and feeling. It can help us express a little more clearly and deeply. Typing is great for writing we want to rework and develop.

day of the week _____ date _____ time _____

location _____ weather _____

My head feels _____

My heart feels _____

My belly feels _____

What my body wants to say right now: _____

_____

_____

_____

_____

_____

[sense writing or freespace] _____

_____

_____

_____

_____

Phrase of the day: _____

What scares me? _____

_____

_____

_____

_____

_____

_____

_____

_____

_____

_____

_____

_____

_____

_____

_____

_____

_____

_____

According to the Online Etymology Dictionary, the earliest words for *write* in most Indo-European languages, which includes English, meant "carve, scratch, cut." In Slavic languages, such as Russian, its origins are related to *paint*.

day of the week _____date _____time_____

location _____weather _____

My head feels _____

My heart feels _____

My belly feels _____

What my body wants to say right now: _____

_____

_____

_____

_____

_____

[sense writing or freespace] _____

_____

_____

_____

_____

_____

Phrase of the day: _____

21

Some of my earliest memories: _____

_____

_____

_____

_____

_____

_____

_____

_____

_____

_____

_____

_____

_____

_____

_____

_____

_____

The words *journal* and *diary* both come from words that mean "day": *jour* in French and *dia* in Spanish. Writing is meant to be daily.

day of the week _____ date _____ time_____

location _____ weather _____

My head feels _____

My heart feels _____

My belly feels _____

What my body wants to say right now: _____

_____

_____

_____

_____

[sense writing or freespace] _____

_____

_____

_____

_____

Phrase of the day: _____

An issue I feel strongly about: _____

_____

_____

_____

_____

_____

_____

_____

_____

_____

_____

_____

_____

_____

_____

_____

_____

_____

_____

_____

There's only one good reason to write: because you want to.

day of the week _____date _____time_____

location _____weather _____

My head feels _____

My heart feels _____

My belly feels _____

What my body wants to say right now: _____

_____

_____

_____

_____

_____

[sense writing or freespace] _____

_____

_____

_____

_____

_____

Phrase of the day: _____

What I like about my life right now: _____

_____

_____

_____

_____

_____

_____

_____

_____

_____

_____

_____

_____

_____

_____

_____

_____

_____

_____

_____

_____

_____

Personal writing is an opportunity to write freely from the perspective of all of our diversities. Every single one of us is a rare and unique combination.

day of the week _____ date _____ time_____

location _____ weather _____

My head feels _____

My heart feels _____

My belly feels _____

What my body wants to say right now: _____

_____

_____

_____

_____

_____

[sense writing or freespace] _____

_____

_____

_____

_____

_____

Phrase of the day: _____

A time I accidentally hurt someone: _____

_____

_____

_____

_____

_____

_____

_____

_____

_____

_____

_____

_____

_____

_____

_____

_____

_____

What does *authentic* mean? It comes from the Greek *autentes*, one who acts on their own authority. When we speak or write with our authentic voice, we know it, and so do others.

68

day of the week _____date _____time_____

location _____weather _____

My head feels _____

My heart feels _____

My belly feels _____

What my body wants to say right now: _____

_____

_____

_____

_____

_____

[sense writing or freespace] _____

_____

_____

_____

_____

_____

Phrase of the day: _____

29

A letter to my seven-year-old self: _____

_____

_____

_____

_____

_____

_____

_____

_____

_____

_____

_____

_____

_____

_____

_____

_____

_____

_____

_____

_____

Writing lets us take a thought and map it out in symbols. It is a code that encapsulates meaning.

Pause & Celebrate

QUEST GOAL REMINDER:
Write daily in these pages for two months.

~~~~~~

It's probably been about a month since you began. Take a moment to think about what you've learned and/or experienced along the way. How's it going? Are you finding your writing rhythms? Did you take some non-writing days? Do you need anything to make it easier to write more regularly?

_____

_____

_____

_____

_____

_____

_____

_____

_____

_____

_____

_____

_____

_____

Write down some of your successes in writing and life recently.

_____

_____

_____

_____

_____

_____

_____

_____

_____

_____

_____

_____

_____

_____

_____

_____

_____

_____

_____

Writing Superpower #3

THE MIND

Our minds are the key to imagination, creative thinking, and language. We can use the mind as a superpower for brainstorming, discerning, reflecting, and self-awareness. A daily practice like writing can help create reliable tracks for our trains of thought.

JUMP-STARTERS TO ACTIVATE THE MIND SUPERPOWER

Imagination
Writers are always stepping into the images their minds see and create. Memories can be reentered and written from another person's perspective or with a different outcome. Writers try out various voices and aspects of their own character (or made-up characters) with distinct points of view.

Thought Trains
What is on that train? What do you think about? Do you ever get bored with your thoughts? Do you tend to talk and write about the same things a lot? There's nothing wrong with that! How often do you entertain new thoughts?

Making Sense

Reflect on our experience, the things that happen, and the people we know. Seek to understand ourselves better. They say you cannot change the past. That's true. But you can change your perspective. And that's timeless. Get curious, and ask yourself what's what. Use the art of awareness and the skills of your intellect (which is just how your brain functions at peak performance—it has nothing to do with education or potential. Everyone has an intellect.).

For the Love of Words!

Make lists of words that intrigue you. Note the way they sound or look or where you read or heard a word for the first time. Think of words only your family or the people in the area where you live say. Experiment with new words. Learn words in other languages.

Beginners Mind

Write ten things you don't know. Ten words you're pretty sure you get wrong. Ten topics or ideas you are interested in. Ten phrases you want to learn in another language.

MIND SUPERPOWER PAGES

Use these pages to explore your Mind Writing Superpower
with one or two of the Jump-Starters on the previous page
or however you want.

_____

_____

_____

_____

_____

_____

_____

_____

_____

_____

_____

_____

_____

_____

_____

_____

_____

_____

_____

_____

_____

day of the week _____ date _____ time_____

location _____ weather _____

What's on my mind right now: _____

_____

_____

Something I saw/did/thought/heard yesterday: _____

_____

_____

_____

_____

_____

_____

Five words to describe my life right now:

_____

_____

_____

_____

_____

Intention for the day: _____

I worry about _____

_____

_____

_____

_____

_____

_____

_____

_____

_____

_____

_____

_____

_____

_____

_____

_____

_____

_____

_____

_____

_____

Writing magically turns thoughts in our head into words on a page.

day of the week _____date _____time_____

location _____weather _____

What's on my mind right now: _____

_____

_____

Something I saw/did/thought/heard yesterday: _____

_____

_____

_____

_____

_____

_____

_____

Five words to describe my life right now:

_____

_____

_____

_____

_____

Intention for the day: _____

34

Who inspires me? Why? _____

_____

_____

_____

_____

_____

_____

_____

_____

_____

_____

_____

_____

_____

_____

_____

_____

_____

_____

_____

A diary/journal/notebook can become a lifelong friend: loyal, reliable, able to keep a secret, there when you need company, nonjudgmental, supportive—and ready to receive everything you have to say, however you want to say it.

day of the week _____ date _____ time_____

location _____ weather _____

What's on my mind right now: _____

_____

_____

Something I saw/did/thought/heard yesterday: _____

_____

_____

_____

_____

_____

_____

Five words to describe my life right now:

_____

_____

_____

_____

Intention for the day: _____

36

Things I wish I could change: _____

_____

_____

_____

_____

_____

_____

_____

_____

_____

_____

_____

_____

_____

_____

_____

_____

_____

_____

_____

_____

There is no right way to write. There is just writing.

day of the week _____ date _____ time_____

location _____ weather _____

What's on my mind right now: _____

_____

_____

Something I saw/did/thought/heard yesterday: _____

_____

_____

_____

_____

_____

Five words to describe my life right now:

_____

_____

_____

_____

Intention for the day: _____

Ten things I would LOVE to do in my life.

1. _____

2. _____

3. _____

4. _____

5. _____

6. _____

7. _____

8. _____

9. _____

10. _____

 One of the oldest diaries still in existence is from eleventh-century
Japan (around one thousand years old), in which Lady Murasaki,
a lady-in-waiting in the imperial court, recorded her daily life.

day of the week _____ date _____ time_____

location _____ weather _____

What's on my mind right now: _____

_____

_____

Something I saw/did/thought/heard yesterday: _____

_____

_____

_____

_____

_____

_____

_____

Five words to describe my life right now:

_____

_____

_____

_____

_____

Intention for the day: _____

In my opinion, _____

_____

_____

_____

_____

_____

_____

_____

_____

_____

_____

_____

_____

_____

_____

_____

_____

_____

_____

_____

Writing is something you practice, like sports, music, or acting. As writing teacher Natalie Goldberg puts it in her book *Writing Down the Bones*, "You practice whether you want to or not. You don't wait around for inspiration and a deep desire. . . ."

day of the week _____ date _____ time_____

location _____ weather _____

What's on my mind right now: _____

_____

_____

Something I saw/did/thought/heard yesterday: _____

_____

_____

_____

_____

_____

_____

_____

Five words to describe my life right now:

_____

_____

_____

_____

_____

Intention for the day: _____

I always _____

_____

_____

I usually _____

_____

_____

I sometimes _____

_____

_____

I rarely _____

_____

_____

I never _____

_____

_____

In the West, the diary as we think of it emerged in the 1800s, when industrial printing presses began to make paper and books available to the average person, and written record-keeping grew more common.

day of the week _____ date _____ time_____

location _____ weather _____

What's on my mind right now: _____

_____

_____

Something I saw/did/thought/heard yesterday: _____

_____

_____

_____

_____

_____

_____

Five words to describe my life right now:

_____

_____

_____

_____

Intention for the day: _____

44

What am I sometimes lazy about? _____

_____

_____

_____

_____

_____

_____

_____

_____

_____

_____

_____

_____

_____

_____

_____

_____

_____

_____

When too many thoughts jostle for your attention, relax and take a breath. Tune in to one word or image that intrigues you. Follow it into a question, a thought, a story. Get curious about what you are saying. Enjoy what you are writing.

Pause & Read

QUEST GOAL REMINDER:
Write daily in these pages for two months.

~~~~~~~~~~~~~~~~~~~~~~~~~

Reading what you've written is usually very interesting. You might find things you forgot you had written, remember something funny, see ways you've changed—or not! Some of it will be boring or embarrassing, or some of it might inspire you.

Take a couple days to reread your first fourteen days of writing. Settle in, relax, and see what you find. It can be fun to reread with colored markers or highlighters and indicate what strikes you, what confuses you, something important, things you like, and anything else.

Don't judge yourself, your thoughts, or your writing. These pages are only for you and belong in a space of compassion. Just because you write something down that you don't like later, it does not define you. It's like a photo that may not show you at your best angle; it's not *you*.

Use these pages to write down the following:

- Your thoughts on what you find
- Words or phrases or sentences that stood out
- Anything else you notice or want to say

Writing Superpower #4

THE HEART

Use this superpower to write into what you feel in your heart. Through our hearts, we know what we love, our emotions, the things we want to express, and the things we believe in. What is your heart open to? What makes it falter? When is it bright? Have you ever had a strong feeling of compassion for someone else?

JUMP-STARTERS TO ACTIVATE THE HEART WRITING SUPERPOWER

The Heart of Intention
Our hearts are where we find our deepest and truest intentions. The inner plans we hold for ourselves. Use this writing time to set a few intentions for the coming year (then mark your calendar to return and read them). Try this prompt: "In my heart of hearts, I intend to . . ."

What I See in You
When we look with our hearts, we tend to see the good in other people. Write down the good you saw in five people you encountered in the last week: friends, families, strangers, or new faces. What happened? What did the person say or do? What surprised you? In what ways are you like this, or want to be more?

Broken-Hearted

There is no way around life's broken hearts. They are part of having relationships with other people, natural disasters, sudden life changes, and the loss of loved ones. Have you had your heart broken? Write down what you would say as a kind and compassionate friend to this part of you that had their heart broken.

Take Your Writer Self on a Date

Think of something your inner writer would love to do, and then take your pages with you and do it. It can be simple and sweet, or a daylong adventure. Step out of your routines and let yourself write somewhere new simply because you love to do it. (P.S. It's normal to feel nervous on a first date!)

Take two days and use the next pages to activate the Heart Writing Superpower. Turn the space into a collage using found papers, images from magazines or newspapers, or photographs.

HEART SUPERPOWER PAGES

Use these pages to explore your Heart Superpower with one or two of the Jump-Starters on the previous page or turn this space into a home of a collage, photo album, poem, song, prayer, or anything else your heart desires.

day of the week _____ date _____ time_____

location _____ weather _____

How I feel right now: _____

_____

_____

What my heart wants to say right now: _____

_____

_____

_____

_____

[freespace] _____

_____

_____

_____

_____

_____

_____

_____

I'm grateful for: _____

The seasons and natural environments I like most: _____

_____

_____

_____

_____

_____

_____

_____

_____

_____

_____

_____

_____

_____

_____

_____

_____

_____

 For centuries, people have turned to private journals in order to document their days, sort out creative problems, help them through crises, comfort them in solitude or pain, or prepare their stories for the future.

—from *The Diary*, an exhibit at the Morgan Library & Museum in New York City.

day of the week _____ date _____ time _____

location _____ weather _____

How I feel right now: _____

_____

_____

What my heart wants to say right now: _____

_____

_____

_____

_____

[freespace] _____

_____

_____

_____

_____

_____

_____

_____

I'm grateful for: _____

Three fields of work I might be interested in:

1. _____

2. _____

3. _____

What is it that interests me about them?

_____

_____

_____

_____

_____

_____

_____

_____

_____

_____

_____

_____

One of the greatest gifts of writing is what we find when we reread our words later. We catch glimpses of ourselves reflected back: some still true, some no longer true.

100

day of the week _____ date _____ time_____

location _____ weather _____

How I feel right now: _____

_____

_____

What my heart wants to say right now: _____

_____

_____

_____

_____

[freespace] _____

_____

_____

_____

_____

_____

_____

_____

_____

I'm grateful for: _____

The earliest dream I remember: _____

_____

_____

_____

_____

_____

_____

_____

_____

_____

_____

_____

_____

_____

_____

_____

In *Dreaming on the Page*, poet and dreamwork professional Tzivia Gover encourages people to write down their nighttime dreams and get curious about unlocking their personal dream language. She says to write our dreams in the present tense. Describe the images in detail. Give the characters names. Make a list of all the verbs. Add more adjectives. How did you feel in the dream and when you woke up?

day of the week _____ date _____ time _____

location _____ weather _____

How I feel right now: _____

_____

_____

What my heart wants to say right now: _____

_____

_____

_____

_____

[freespace] _____

_____

_____

_____

_____

_____

_____

_____

_____

I'm grateful for: _____

A time I had to say goodbye to someone, something, or someplace:

_____

_____

_____

_____

_____

_____

_____

_____

_____

_____

_____

_____

_____

_____

_____

_____

In *Writing the Mind Alive*, Linda Trichter Metcalf teaches a unique writing practice to really listen to and engage with what you are writing. When a word catches your attention, write this exact phrase: "What do I mean by [the word or phrase]?" Give expression to what the word means specifically to you, the images, memories, and associations. Follow the trail. You may do this once or several times in one writing session. The page always wants to know more.

day of the week _____date _____time_____

location _____weather _____

How I feel right now: _____

_____

_____

What my heart wants to say right now: _____

_____

_____

_____

_____

[freespace] _____

_____

_____

_____

_____

_____

_____

I'm grateful for: _____

How can I develop my uniqueness? _____

_____

_____

_____

_____

_____

_____

_____

_____

_____

_____

_____

_____

_____

_____

_____

_____

_____

For fun, go back to the list from #38 and cross out five of them. Keep the five that are most important, interesting, or motivating to you. If you want to add new ones, go ahead, but you'll have to cross off others so only five remain.

day of the week _____ date _____ time_____

location _____ weather _____

How I feel right now: _____
_____
_____

What my heart wants to say right now: _____
_____
_____
_____
_____

[freespace] _____
_____
_____
_____
_____
_____
_____
_____
_____

I'm grateful for: _____

In what ways am I a rebel? In what ways do I want to be?

_____

_____

_____

_____

_____

_____

_____

_____

_____

_____

_____

_____

_____

_____

_____

_____

_____

_____

_____

Now, go to the list from #38 and from the five that are left, put a star next to the three things that are the most important to you. Cross off the other two. Write the three that remain on page 153.

day of the week _____date _____time_____

location _____weather _____

How I feel right now: _____

_____

_____

What my heart wants to say right now: _____

_____

_____

_____

_____

[freespace] _____

_____

_____

_____

_____

_____

_____

_____

I'm grateful for: _____

A letter to my twenty-one-year-old self:

Dear _____

_____

_____

_____

_____

_____

_____

_____

_____

_____

_____

_____

_____

_____

_____

_____

_____

_____

_____

_____

_____

_____

_____

_____

Finally, from the list from #38 you have three things left. Now, put them in order of importance to you. Write the three things on page 153.

Congratulations!

You did it. You've officially reached the end of the quest.

You now have a lot of pages with your words, ideas, stories, opinions, and more. You also have a ton of writing cues and templates and superpowers to continue your writing journey. Most important, you have the experience (and hopefully satisfaction) of setting out on a personal quest and achieving your goal—however you got here!

Write yourself a congratulations note.

_____

_____

_____

_____

_____

_____

_____

_____

_____

_____

_____

_____

Make a Wish

It is said that a person should tuck away special memories, dreams, and wishes in their heart, like gems in a treasure chest that only they have the key to. Take a moment now to feel into your heart and make a wish to look back on down the road. You can write it here: _____

_____

_____

_____

_____

_____

_____

_____

_____

_____

_____

_____

_____

_____

_____

_____

_____

_____

_____

QUEST GOAL REMINDER:
Write daily in these pages for two months.

Start date (from page 12): _____   Today's date: _____

About how long did I take to write through these pages?

_____

_____

_____

WRITING AS AN OASIS:
a daily writing habit that cultivates an inner feeling of comfort,
no matter what's going on around you

HOW MANY OF THESE WERE TRUE FOR ME AS I MADE MY WAY
THROUGH THE OASIS PAGES?

◯ I wanted to write.

◯ I remembered to write.

◯ I had everything I needed to write (pens, paper).

◯ I found/created time.

◯ I enjoyed it.

◯ Writing helped me in ways that matter.

◯ I did it for me.

Which do I prefer?

Open-ended invitations   Specific prompts   My own thing

How confident do you feel about being about to write daily in the future?

Of course   Very   Pretty confident   Somewhat   Not very

Do you want to continue a writing habit?

Of course   Yes   I might   Maybe   Probably not

Do you think you could use the Oasis Pages approach to something else you'd like to accomplish?

Of course   Yes   Maybe   Not sure   Probably not

What other "quests" might you like to take? What might you want to learn or do or change or experience, now in your life, soonish, down the road, in the future? _____

_____

_____

_____

_____

_____

Reflection

The goal of the Oasis Pages is not the most important thing. It is the experience of the quest itself. You cannot win a quest. You can only achieve the goal you set out to accomplish. The treasures, the true gifts of a quest, lie in reflecting on the inner journey.

What have I learned about myself from this experience?

_____

_____

_____

_____

_____

_____

_____

_____

_____

_____

_____

_____

_____

_____

_____

_____

_____

_____

You are unique.

Your words are important.

Your voice matters.

Keep On Writing

Now that you have a daily writing habit, use it on some blank pages. On the following pages, it's up to you to keep a daily writing habit going. You can draw on cues and prompts from earlier pages or do your own thing. Start an essay or novel. Experiment with what works for you.

If you're stuck for what to write about, draw on your Writing Superpowers: Curiosity, the Body, the Mind, and the Heart. Or take an idea from the prompts, questions, and topics in the Jump-Starters section. There are also the feelings words from page 20 (see the prompts at the bottom).

Pro Tips

Date your entries—it can be frustrating later when you want to know when you wrote something.

Think about what tools you need for writing and get your next journal/diary/notebook. Not having the materials you need for writing is a prime way that a writing habit can get dropped. There are a lot of options out there. Find the size and shape that works for you.

Struggling with writing but want to? Jump to page 154 for more ideas.

Enjoy your writing journey.
Make time to visit your inner oasis.
Keep on questing.

_____
_____
_____
_____
_____
_____
_____
_____
_____
_____
_____
_____
_____
_____

"*So do not fear your fear. Own it. Free it. This isn't a liberation that I or anyone can give you—it's a power you must look for, learn, love, lead, and locate for yourself.*"
—Amanda Gorman, poet and advocate

_____

_____

_____

_____

_____

_____

_____

_____

_____

_____

_____

_____

_____

_____

_____

_____

_____

_____

_____

_____

"Privacy, like eating and breathing, is one
of life's basic requirements."

—Katherine Neville, author

_____

_____

_____

_____

_____

_____

_____

_____

_____

_____

_____

_____

_____

_____

_____

_____

"Write what should not be forgotten."
—Isabel Allende, novelist and journalist

_____

_____

_____

_____

_____

_____

_____

_____

_____

_____

_____

_____

_____

_____

_____

_____

_____

_____

_____

_____

"Life is either a daring adventure or nothing."
—Helen Keller, author and advocate

_____

_____

_____

_____

_____

_____

_____

_____

_____

_____

_____

_____

_____

_____

_____

_____

*"I think the act of writing cleanses me of the day's
stresses; a problem always seems smaller once it's
written down."*

—Claire Hamilton, radio journalist

_____

_____

_____

_____

_____

_____

_____

_____

_____

_____

_____

_____

_____

_____

_____

_____

_____

_____

_____

_____

"All we have to do is to wake up and change."
—Greta Thunberg, teen Earth advocate

_____

_____

_____

_____

_____

_____

_____

_____

_____

_____

_____

_____

_____

_____

"Writing is one of the most ancient forms of prayer."
—Fatima Mernissi, writer, sociologist, advocate

_____

_____

_____

_____

_____

_____

_____

_____

_____

_____

_____

_____

_____

_____

_____

_____

_____

_____

_____

_____

"We all live with the objective of being happy; our lives are all different and yet the same."

—Anne Frank, diarist

_____

_____

_____

_____

_____

_____

_____

_____

_____

_____

_____

_____

_____

_____

_____

_____

_____

_____

_____

_____

_____

_____

"In nature, nothing is perfect and everything is perfect. Trees can be contorted, bent in weird ways, and they're still beautiful."

—Alice Walker, poet, author, advocate

_____

_____

_____

_____

_____

_____

_____

_____

_____

_____

_____

_____

_____

_____

_____

_____

_____

_____

_____

_____

_____

_____

"I want kids to learn that, yes, it's okay
to acknowledge that you're good or even
great at something."

—Simone Biles, gymnast and Olympic gold medalist

_____

_____

_____

_____

_____

_____

_____

_____

_____

_____

_____

_____

_____

_____

_____

"What you do makes a difference, and you have to decide what kind of difference you want to make."
—Jane Goodall, humanitarian and animal advocate

_____

_____

_____

_____

_____

_____

_____

_____

_____

_____

_____

_____

_____

_____

_____

_____

_____

_____

_____

_____

_____

"We realize the importance of our voices
only when we are silenced."

—Malala Yousafzai, educator and advocate

_____

_____

_____

_____

_____

_____

_____

_____

_____

_____

_____

_____

_____

_____

_____

"*I wanted to write stories for myself. . . . I just wanted to become good at the art of something. And writing was very private.*"

—Amy Tan, novelist

_____

_____

_____

_____

_____

_____

_____

_____

_____

_____

_____

_____

_____

_____

_____

_____

_____

_____

_____

_____

_____

"The hardest times for me were not when people challenged what I said, but when I felt my voice was not heard."

—Carol Gilligan, psychologist, author, advocate

_____

_____

_____

_____

_____

_____

_____

_____

_____

_____

_____

_____

_____

_____

"I think, at a child's birth, if a mother could ask a fairy godmother to endow it with the most useful gift, that gift should be curiosity."
—Eleanor Roosevelt, former first lady of the United States

There is a vitality, a life force, an energy, a quickening that is translated through you into action, and because there is only one of you in all of time, this expression is unique. And if you block it, it will never exist through any other medium and will be lost.

—Martha Graham, choreographer

_____

_____

_____

_____

_____

_____

_____

_____

_____

_____

_____

_____

_____

_____

_____

_____

"Each of us has an inner dream that we can unfold if we will just have the courage to admit what it is. And the faith to trust our own admission."
—Julia Cameron, creativity author

Three things I would LOVE to do in my life
(from page 109)

1. _____

2. _____

3. _____

Three things I would LOVE to do in my life
(from page 111)

1. _____

2. _____

3. _____

BONUS RESOURCES

Everyone struggles to write sometimes. When writing becomes a challenge, consider the thoughts below. Also try out the Writing Jump-Starters on pages 156–157 anytime!

Be kind with yourself.
Maybe writing is not the right thing for you or it's not the right time. Whatever is going on, have compassion. Luckily, the page is always there and when you are ready.

Write with others.
Sometimes writing with someone else or a small group feels good and can help bring energy to our writing habit. You don't have to read what each person has written. Just set a time and place, say hello, write, share a little about the experience (not the writing), say goodbye. Look for a teen community writing classes.

Experiment with larger chunks of time.
Some people need a lot of time to write a whole lot of pages. Try setting aside an afternoon, day, or weekend. Then write, write, write. Maybe have a backup notebook or journal. Whether it's pent-up personal stories, emotions, experiences, or a new idea for a creative project, a character, or place— write it down. Sometimes writing comes in torrents.

Called to paper but not writing?

Then draw, sketch, doodle, or collage. Try learning origami, or keep a scrapbook.

Called to writing but not personal writing?

Then write characters, short stories, novels, poems. Create a one-person show or an open-mic script. Play with language and create quizzes and puzzles.

Writing not for you?

Just as dance isn't for everyone, neither is a writing practice. The important thing is to find the life-positive things that work for you and engage the Body, the Mind, and the Heart. Sports? Painting? Singing? Building things? Getting people together? Fishing? Yoga? Tap into whatever it is that helps you feel sane, relaxed, and happy, that gives you energy and brings you life. Even if you don't write anymore, you have this book to look back on.

OASIS PAGES
WRITING JUMP-STARTERS
When you're not sure what to write, these ideas can get you going.

Prompts
I believe . . .
I just don't like . . .
I remember . . .
I don't remember . . .
I want . . .
A nice thing someone said about me . . .

Questions
What kinds of things do I like to do outdoors?
Do I tend to stand out or fit in?
What's my relationship with food?
Do I believe in miracles?
What things make me unhappy?
Which school subjects interest me? Which don't?

Topics
Personal: you, you, you—anything and everything!
Love: How do you know? In love now or been in love?
Do tell . . .
School: Like it/love it/hate it? College?
Volunteer work: Do you? Would you? What kind?

Write a letter to . . .

Someone you admire

Someone who hurt you

Your body

The stars above

My list

What topics, people, events, experiences do you want to write about?

_____   _____

_____   _____

_____   _____

_____   _____

_____   _____

_____   _____

_____   _____

_____   _____

_____   _____

Dear Writer,

Here is the first diary entry I ever wrote, in pencil and dated Friday, May 30. I was ten.

> Dear Diary,
> today was cloudy *sunny
> today I got my tonsils taken out.
> It hurts a lot.
> I got them taken out at Iidea E Hall.
> I was scared.

In pen, written at a later point: *"That's where I was born."*

I like the simplicity and honesty of my thoughts. I love that I went back and edited the entry later. That small one-year diary lasted me five years—and was still half empty when I rediscovered it many years later! No one told me how to write, so I just showed up once in a while and wrote things like what I got for my birthday or who I had a crush on or something that happened at school.

I wish I had had a writing quest with prompts, questions, and tips to write down other aspects of myself and my life, questions I had, what I thought about, the things that worried me, my hopes and dreams, my secrets. So when I grew up, I created the Oasis Pages for you.

My advice is to develop a habit of curiosity. About yourself, your life, your writing ways, anything that interests you or bothers you! Everyone needs a place where they can think freely and be themselves, an inner oasis. Writing is mine. Maybe it's yours, too.

Warmly,

Grace

Library of Congress Cataloging-in-Publication Data available.
ISBN: 978-1-68555-017-2
LCCN: 2022906482

Printed using Forest Stewardship Council certified stock
from sustainably managed forests.

Manufactured in China.

Design by Regina Shklovsky.

1 3 5 7 9 10 8 6 4 2

The Collective Book Studio®
Oakland, California
www.thecollectivebook.studio